WHY DO TRAINS STAY ON TRACK?

TRAIN BOOKS FOR KIDS

CHILDREN'S TRANSPORTATION BOOKS

Speedy Publishing LLC
40 E. Main St. #1156
Newark, DE 19711
www.speedypublishing.com

In this book, we're going to talk about why trains stay on their tracks. So, let's get right to it!

In the days before cars and airplanes, people had limited options on how to get across larger distances. Horse-drawn carriages moved people and goods, but they were limited by the roads that were available, and they struggled during bad weather.

As early as 1550, people in Germany began building and using railway systems made of wood. They reasoned that wagons and carts could travel more easily if they used wooden rails instead of unpaved roads.

By the end of the 1700s, wheels and rails made of iron had replaced the wooden ones. Once the invention of the steam locomotive was introduced in England in 1797, the concept of a railway with train engines pulling cars became a possibility.

Steam Engine

Some of the first locomotives powered by steam could haul up to 450 passengers and 6 supply cars filled with coal over a distance of about 9 miles in less than 1 hour. Horses couldn't compete with the "iron horse."

HOW ARE TRAIN TRACKS CONSTRUCTED?

Trains get from one place to another on tracks. The tracks provide a surface that is low-friction. The tracks guide the train engine and its attached cars and transfer the train's weight to the ground under it. If the train is run by electricity, there is a third rail that provides electrical power.

740

If you look carefully at the tracks of a railway, you'll notice that it is made of two steel rails that are parallel to each other. In order for these rails to stay parallel to each other, they must always stay a fixed distance apart. This fixed distance is called the gauge. The gauge is set at a standard distance of 4 feet, 8 1/2 inches or 1,435 millimeters.

It's a legend that this gauge was based on the width of a Roman chariot, but it isn't true. Chariots were used as fighting machines not as a way to move supplies. George Stephenson, who was the British inventor who created the very first system for railways, is the one who specified this standard.

To ensure that the parallel steel rails stay the correct distance apart, ties made either of wood or sometimes of concrete are bolted to the rails. In Europe, these ties are called "sleepers." The ties or sleepers are set into loose stones or gravel. These loose stones are called "ballast." The ballast helps the weight of the load to transfer to the foundation below it. The ties are "floating" on top of the loose stones and the track keeps them from moving too much.

The tracks are usually elevated above the ground that surrounds them so that if there's water it will drain away from the tracks. Sometimes there are fences to prevent stray animals from walking over the tracks. If the train runs on electricity, there will an electric power rail or wires that overhang above the train to supply the train with electricity.

Depending on the topography of the land, whether it's flat or hilly, the tracks will be either straight or curved. Some curved tracks will be angled to help the train stay on the rails as it goes around the curve.

SWITCHES AND SIGNALS

At places along the track, there are switches that allow a train to move from one track to another. These switches are important when two trains are traveling on the same track. A switch allows a train to pull off the main track onto a special area with a holding track so that another train can pass.

Switches can also change the direction that a train is moving. For example, if a train is traveling on a track that is traveling north to south, a switch can change the train's direction so that it's traveling from east to west.

72

Some railroad stations have special yards that are designed as switching yards. There, trains are moved to different tracks and re-assembled in different ways.

SRT
1132

There are also signals along the train tracks that provide information to the operators of the trains so they are aware of upcoming traffic situations. These signals work like the traffic signals for traffic of automobiles on roadways.

In addition to these signals, some train engines have radio or computer dashboards that monitor the region's traffic using signals sent out by a central information hub. This communication system to relay information about train traffic is similar to how an air traffic control center works for airplanes.

Train Dashboard

HOW ARE TRAIN WHEELS CONSTRUCTED?

Trains move very fast along their tracks and unlike cars no one steers them. If you look at a photo of train tracks, you'll notice that when tracks go around a curve the outer rail has a curving radius that's larger than the curving radius of the inner rail. In order to stay on track and follow the turn on the tracks, the wheels on the outer edge have to move faster than the wheels on the inner edge.

One possible method to make the outer wheels move more quickly than the inner ones would be to make the inner wheels smaller than the outer ones. However, that wouldn't solve the problem because then we could only turn in the same direction as the direction that has the smaller wheels. If the right wheels are smaller, we could turn to the right and if the left wheels are smaller we could turn to the left.

However, since we have to go both right and left at different times this would never work. Also, a train that had unequally sized wheels couldn't travel on a straight level track.

A car has this same problem too, but it has a device called a differential. It makes it possible for the outside wheels to turn faster than the inside wheels when the car is turning. Trains don't have this type of device because their wheels have a very ingenious design that allows the trains to travel in either direction on a curved track.

The wheels on a train are slanted with the larger dimensions facing each other and the smaller dimensions facing out. If you took an orange plastic cone and chopped off the bottom four inches of it and threw the rest away, it would give you an idea of the three-dimensional look of a train's wheel. Do the same thing with two plastic cones and then face them together with their larger dimensions facing each other. Now you'll have a good model for how a train's wheels work.

When the track is straight, the center of each wheel is making contact with the rails at the exact same distance so the train travels straight forward. If the train begins to make a right turn, the rails are guiding it to do so and the rails are turning right.

FABLOK
SM42
764
850kN

The outside wheel, which is the left one in this case, would begin to go off the rail. Its left portion, which is its smaller dimension would begin to lose touch with the rails while its right side would remain in touch.

The same thing would happen with the right wheel. Its left side would begin losing contact with the rails while its right side would remain in contact. In other words, the left sides of each of the wheels lose contact with the rails because the train as well as the rails are turning right.

35010

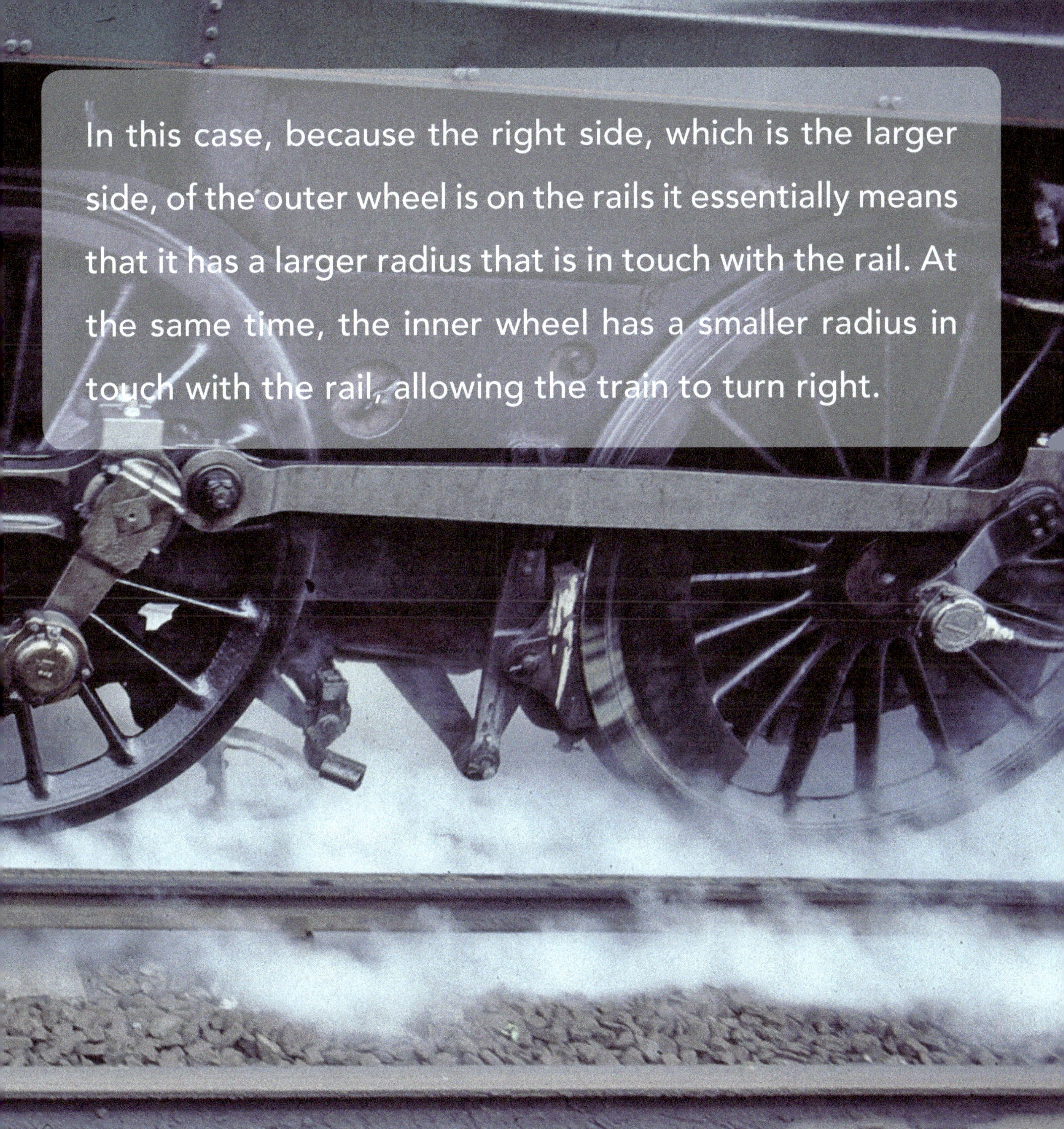

In this case, because the right side, which is the larger side, of the outer wheel is on the rails it essentially means that it has a larger radius that is in touch with the rail. At the same time, the inner wheel has a smaller radius in touch with the rail, allowing the train to turn right.

This wheel design accomplishes exactly the same thing as if we had two wheels of different sizes. The outer wheels have a higher velocity since their radius of contact is higher. The inner wheels have a lower velocity because their radius of contact with the rails is smaller.

WASHINGTON
88
ROGERS

Of course, if the train is turning left the exact opposite will happen. It will shift so the wheel on the left has the smaller radius in contact and the wheel on the right will have the larger radius. It's important for the train tracks to turn very gradually so that the train wheels can accommodate for the turn. The driver doesn't have anything to do with turning the train!

SUMMARY

Trains stay on track using steel rails that are parallel to each other. These steel rails are bolted together with ties so they remain in place over a foundation of loose stones. The steel rails can be straight or curved depending on what type of terrain the train must cover.

In order for the train to turn, the rails must go into a gradual, not a steep, turn. The wheels have a special tapered design that allows them to stay on the track whether the train is traveling straight or turning right or left.

Awesome! Now that you've read about why trains stay on their tracks, you may want to read about trucks, trains and big machines in the Baby Professor book ***Trucks, Trains and Big Machines! Transportation Books for Kids.***

Visit
BABY PROFESSOR
EDUCATION KIDS
www.BabyProfessorBooks.com
to download Free Baby Professor eBooks
and view our catalog of new and exciting
Children's Books

www.ingramcontent.com/pod-product-compliance
Lightning Source LLC
LaVergne TN
LVHW060829170826
845678LV00010B/1933

* 9 7 9 8 8 6 9 4 3 4 7 5 3 *